Tapping into the Love

From the Heart of God

By Linda J.B. Williford

Cover Design: Dennis Carroll
Photo Front Cover: Tamas/Dreamstime.com
Editor: Katherine R. Mandy

Scripture quotations taken from The Holy Bible, New
International Version ® NIV ® Copyright ©1973, 1978,
1984, 2011 by Biblica, Inc. ® Used by permission. All
rights reserved worldwide.

ISBN: 978-0-9704718-3-3

I dedicate this book to all who desire to know God and His amazing, awesome love.

May you come into the Presence of God through His Holy Scriptures and receive an understanding of how the Heavenly Father loves you more than you will ever know.

As you read this devotional, be blessed beyond your expectations as you are **Tapping into the Love.**

Table of Contents

Introduction

From the Very Beginning

In the Book of Genesis, the Bible tells of the miraculous creation of the world. God created the heavens and the earth. He then created the first humans, Adam and Eve. *"So, God created mankind in his own image, in the image of God he created them; male and female he created them"* (Genesis 1:27). They were to be fruitful and multiply and to rule over God's magnificent world.

God created them to have a happy and beautiful life. He created them to have a divine relationship with Him. This could have been a "happy ever after" story. Everything was perfect until sin came into the picture.

The Bible tells us that Adam and Eve were created with a free will. They had the ability to make choices. Unfortunately, they chose to disobey God by eating the only fruit that God forbid them to eat in the Garden of Eden. That disobedience led to a broken relationship with God. This was the fall of man. All the descendants of Adam and Eve, which unfortunately includes you and me, are born under the curse of sin.

But here is the Good News! God did not give up on man and woman because of their disobedience. He still wanted that relationship with His creation.

The Bible tells us: *"For God so loved the world that he gave his one and only Son, that whoever believes in him should not perish but have eternal life"* John 3:16.

God provided the way for us to be redeemed and to be restored back to Him. He also gave each of us a free will to make choices. We can believe in Jesus, God's gift to the world, or live a life without God. It's our choice.

The Scriptures in this devotional book will help you experience the love of God so that you can have the relationship that our Heavenly Father wanted from the very beginning of time.

Notes & Reflections

Day 1

"....to grasp how wide and long and high and deep is the love of Christ....that you may be filled to the measure of all the fullness of God."
Ephesians 3:18-19

God's Love – Deep and Wide

Can we truly comprehend the love of God?
It surpasses our human knowledge and understanding.
It's beyond what we can grasp. It's too wide and too deep.

The Bible tells us that nothing can separate us
from this love. *"...death nor life, angels nor demons, present nor future, nor powers, height nor depth, nor anything else in all creation..."* Romans 8:38-39.

Why does Jesus Christ love us this much? We surely
don't deserve it. Jesus wants us to experience
the fullness of God and all that He is. He wants us
to know the Father God of all creation.
Receive this love that will
change your heart and life forever.

Tap into the Love...

Prayer: Father God, I want Your love that I don't
understand. Cleanse me from my sins and receive
me now as your child, so that I can experience Your
awesome love. In the name of Jesus, Amen.

Notes & Reflections

Day 2

"And being found in appearance as a man, he humbled himself by becoming obedient to death—even death on a cross!"
Philippians 2:8

Jesus Demonstrated God's Love

Jesus came down to earth from His heavenly throne to become man. Jesus obeyed and honored the Father by closing the gap of sin between man and God.

Jesus demonstrated that love by going to the Cross. Jesus said that no man takes His life from Him, *"but I lay it down of my own accord. I have authority to lay it down and authority to take it up again"* John 10:18.

Jesus paid the price for us all. Now we need to demonstrate our love to God by loving and serving others in the name of Jesus.

Tap into the Love....

Prayer: Thank you, Jesus, for dying for me so that I could have eternal life with You and the Heavenly Father. Help me to spread the Good News and love to others. Amen.

Notes & Reflections

Day 3

"If you love me, keep my commands.
And I will ask the Father, and he will give you
another advocate to help you and be with you
forever—the Spirit of truth."
John 14:15-17

The Spirit of Truth

Jesus was preparing His disciples for when He would be leaving to go back to heaven. Now the Spirit of Truth, also known as the Holy Spirit, would come to live within them. He would be their constant companion.

The Holy Spirit is part of the Deity of God. God the Father, God the Son, and God the Holy Spirit. All three in One. *"For in Christ all the fullness of the Deity lives in bodily form, and in Christ you have been brought to fullness" Colossians 2:9-10.*

The Holy Spirit interprets the Scriptures for us. He helps with our weaknesses. He is our counselor and intercedes for us. He is our daily reminder and guide. Ask the Holy Spirit to show you the way today.

Tap into the Love...

Prayer: Father God, thank you that I'm never alone. You are always with me through the Holy Spirit. I can always call on You through the beautiful name of Jesus. Amen.

Notes & Reflections

Day 4

"All Scripture is God-breathed and is useful for teaching, rebuking, correcting and training in righteousness, so that the servant of God may be thoroughly equipped for every good work."
2 Timothy 3:16-17

The Living Word

The Holy Scriptures are inspired by God. They are full of wisdom and guidance. They reveal the mysteries of God. His Word helps us fight our battles with the enemy of this world.

Jesus said when He was tempted by Satan, *"It is written: Man shall not live on bread alone, but on every word that comes from the mouth of God"* Matthew 4:4.

As you read and study the Word of God, you will discover new things as God will not only reveal himself to you but also reveal His plan for your life. We need to feed on the living word everyday.

Tap into the Love...

Prayer: Lord God, help me to be spiritually equipped for every good work by receiving nourishment from Your Holy Word daily. Amen.

Notes & Reflections

Day 5

*"For you are a people holy to the Lord your God.
Out of all the peoples on the face of the earth, the
Lord has chosen you to be his treasured possession."*
Deuteronomy 14:2

We Have Been Chosen

God told the children of Israel that they were His
treasured possession. Did you know that
we are His treasured possession, too?

God offered His Son, Jesus Christ, to all peoples
of the world so that all might be saved. Go to Romans
Chapter 8 and read verses 14 to17 to learn how we have
been adopted into the family of God.

We are precious jewels to God. We have been chosen.
Take time to know God's love. Thank Him that you are
one of His treasured possessions.

Tap into the Love...

Prayer: Dear Father God, help me to realize how precious
I am in Your sight. You say that whosoever will come to
You , You will receive, and they will become a child
of Yours. Thank you for loving me. Amen.

Notes & Reflections

Day 6

"The Spirit you received...brought about your adoption to sonship. And by him we cry, 'Abba, Father.' The Spirit himself testifies with our spirit that we are God's children." Romans 8:15-16

Abba, Our Father

From the very beginning of time, God has always wanted to live among His people and be their God. Jesus provided the way it could happen.

The Scriptures say, *"I will be a Father to you, and you will be my sons and daughters, says the Lord Almighty"* 2 Corinthians 6:18.

Our Lord God wants us to depend upon Him like a child would a parent. Whatever is bothering you today, call upon the Heavenly Father. He knows best and will answer with unconditional love.

Tap into the Love...

Prayer: Dear Father God, I am so thankful that I can cry out, Abba, Father, to You. I trust in You with a child's heart that You will answer. You know what is best for me. In Jesus' name, Amen.

Notes & Reflections

Day 7

*"He heals the brokenhearted and
binds up their wounds."*
Psalms 147:3

_____.

Comfort for the Brokenhearted

Our hearts can be broken for many reasons.
We can be attacked from every facet of life: mentally,
physically, or spiritually.

The pain hurts to the inner core of the soul.
But Jesus came to heal broken people.
"The Lord is close to the brokenhearted and saves
those who are crushed in spirit" Psalms 34:18.

Is your heart breaking today? Lay your pain at the
feet of Jesus. Humbly wait for His touch. He will give you
comfort and peace. He will turn your broken heart into a
joyful heart. Receive His love and healing.

Tap into the Love...

Prayer: Lord Jesus, I give you my broken heart. Thank
you that You came to comfort and to heal. I now
receive Your love and healing. Amen.

Notes & Reflections

Day 8

"He will cover you with his feathers, and under his wings you will find refuge; his faithfulness will be your shield and rampart."
Psalms 91:4

Snuggled Under His Wings

Imagine this ….God pulling you up close to Him, safely under His wings. Sometimes we need that visual and to be reminded that the Lord is always there for us. His faithfulness is our shield.

The Bible tells us that there will always be troubles in this world. But it also tells us, *"….the Lord's unfailing love surrounds the one who trusts in him"* Psalm 32:10. What a beautiful promise.

Praise God for His loving kindness and His faithfulness. Allow the Lord to pull you close and snuggle you safely under His wings. Find peace and safety in a loving God who cares for you.

Tap into the Love…

Prayer: Dear Father God, You are awesome! I praise you and worship you with a grateful heart. Amen

Notes & Reflections

Day 9

*"You will seek me and find me when you
seek me with all your heart."*
Jeremiah 29:13

A Daily Habit

Develop a habit of waking up each morning, or whatever
time of the day is best for you, to have some quiet time with
God. Ask God what He would say to you for the day. What
does He want you to know? What does He want you to do?

Anticipate an answer from God as you pray and reflect
from your daily Scripture readings. As you seek the
Lord, He promises that you WILL find him.
Be quiet and listen. *The Lord is my portion;
therefore, I will wait for him"* Lamentations 3:24.

There is nothing more satisfying to the soul and more
peaceful to the mind than to know that God has seen your
heart and is guiding you throughout the day.

Tap into the Love...

Prayer: Father God, I love you and seek you with all my
heart. I wait to hear from You and to receive Your
blessings that You have for me today. Amen.

Notes & Reflections

Day 10

"But Moses said, "Pardon your servant, Lord.
Please send someone else."
Exodus 4:13

The Calling

When God gave the assignment for Moses to lead the
children of Israel out of Egypt, Moses experienced
self-doubt, uncertainty, and hesitancy.

Exodus Chapters 3 and 4 give the account of God
calling Moses. Note that God's will is never forced upon
anyone. God operates from a foundation of love. With
Moses' insecurities, God called Aaron to help
Moses with the mission.

When we are called to do a mission for God,
we may find ourselves inadequate for the job.
However, God is good. He takes into consideration our
insecurities and limitations and provides a way
for us to accomplish His purpose.

Tap into the Love...

Prayer: Father God, thank you for loving me in spite
of all my insecurities. Thank you for accepting me just as
I am. Thank you for giving me the grace and the help I need
to accomplish Your purpose. Amen

Notes & Reflections

Day 11

"For I am the Lord your God who takes hold
of your right hand and says to you,
Do not fear; I will help you."
Isaiah 41:13

Overcoming Fear

Have you noticed that "fear" is addressed numerous times throughout the Old and New Testaments? Obviously, we humans are creatures of fear.

The Scriptures tell us that the author of fear is Satan. *"Be alert and of a sober mind. Your enemy the devil prowls around like a roaring lion looking for someone to devour"* 1 Peter 5:8.

But God did not give us a spirit of fear. Instead, He gave us the Spirit of love. And perfect love drives away fear. (I John 4:18) Ask the Father to give you that love which overcomes fear.

Tap into the Love…

Prayer: Father God, help me to have courage when I am fearful. Help me to trust You because I know greater are You who is within me than he that is in the world. Amen

Notes & Reflections

Day 12

"If we confess our sins, God is faithful and just
and will forgive us our sins and purify us
from all unrighteousness."
1 John 1:9

Oops! When We Sin

We all have intentions of being good, but sometimes,
we just mess up. The Bible plainly tells us that when
we sin, confess it to our faithful and forgiving God.

We have the assurance from God that all sins are
removed from us *"as far as the east is from the west"*
Psalms 103:12. Trust God. There is no
condemnation but forgiveness.

Repent of the sin that is stealing your peace and joy.
Receive God's forgiveness and be restored
to that awesome relationship
with your Heavenly Father once again.

Tap into the Love...

Prayer: Father God, thank you for Your amazing
grace of forgiveness. Thank you for forgiving
me when I mess up. Amen

Notes & Reflections

Day 13

*"God made him who had no sin to be sin for us, so
that in him we might become
the righteousness of God."*
2 Corinthians 5:21

Know Who You Are

By accepting Jesus as Lord of your life, you are now
becoming the righteousness of God.
God loves us and has promised to protect His own.

When you suffer trials and tribulations, remember this
verse: *"And we know that in all things
God works for the good of those who
love him...."* Roman 8:28. God has a way of
turning bad things into good things.

Know who you are in Christ. You are the
righteousness of God. Thank Jesus for His
amazing love who made that possible for you.

Tap into the Love...

Prayer: Father God, when troubles come my way, help me to
remember who I am in Christ. Your love and Your
protection is always with me. Thank you. Amen

Notes & Reflections

Day 14

*"The prayer of a righteous person
is powerful and effective."*
James 5:16

The Righteous Prayers

We normally don't see ourselves as righteous persons.
Righteousness is defined as being upright or moral.
God wants us to live upright, honorable lives
and to be moral. Do right in all things.

If we live a righteous life, God will listen to our prayers.
*"For the eyes of the Lord are on the righteous and his
ears are attentive to their prayer...."* 1 Peter 3:12.

The Scriptures tell us to pray constantly. Who or what do
you need to be praying for today? It's easier to pray when
you know your prayers are powerful and effective.

Tap into the Love...

Prayer: Dear Lord, forgive me from any sin
that may be hindering my prayers from being
powerful and effective. Amen

Notes & Reflections

Day 15

"But God has surely listened and has heard my prayer. Praise be to God, who has not rejected my prayer or withheld his love from me."
Psalms 66:19-20

God Does Listen

If you give it some thought, it's almost impossible to have a truly intimate relationship with God ....without waiting. The Bible is full of people who had to wait on God.

The Lord uses all the time necessary to prepare our hearts and the hearts of others before He answers our prayers. *"Be still before the Lord and wait patiently for him"* Psalm 37:7.

One day you will be able to proclaim like the Psalmist David that God did listen and did answer your prayer. God's timing is always perfect. Trust Him.

Tap into the Love...

Prayer: Father God, I thank you for hearing my requests. I believe in Your perfect timing. You are good and will not withhold Your love from me. Amen

Notes & Reflections

Day 16

"I urge.....that petitions, prayers, intercession
and thanksgiving be made for all people."
1 Timothy 2:1

Intercessory Prayer

When you pray for someone, consider this: Prayer is like
transacting business with God on that person's behalf. We
ask God to take that person's best interest into
consideration.

The Scriptures tell us in Ephesians 3:16
that our Lord not only heals the physical needs
but will also strengthen the inner being through
the miraculous power of the Holy Spirit.

Ask God to heal the whole person. Ask God
to heal the physical, as well as the spiritual, needs of that
person for whom you are interceding.

Tap into the Love...

Prayer: Father God, help me to see the prayer of
intercession as another way of helping
my neighbor and those I love. Amen

Notes & Reflections

Day 17

"He got up, rebuked the wind and said to the waves, 'Quiet! Be still!' Then the wind died down and it was completely calm."
Mark 4:39

Storms of the Mind

Our minds can take us to dangerous places of thoughts, fear, and panic. These things can create an uncontrollable raging storm from within us.

Jesus controlled the furious storm in which He and the disciples were suddenly caught. Afterwards, Jesus asked the disciples, *"Why are you so afraid? Do you still have no faith?"* Mark 4:40

All things obey when Jesus speaks. You can call upon His name in the midst of your storms. He will quiet and calm the storms of your mind as well as any other storms that you may face.

Tap into the Love...

Prayer: Lord God, when the storms are raging from within or from the outside, help me to believe in Your power. You are in control of all things. Give me quiet and peace of mind. Amen

Notes & Reflections

Day 18

*"Whether you turn to the right or to the left, your
ears will hear a voice behind you, saying,
'This is the way; walk in it."*
Isaiah 30:21

Whispers of God

We need to recognize the Spirit of God
when He nudges and speaks to us. And in order to do
that, we must stay attuned to God through prayer
and His Holy Scriptures.

"He says, "Be still, and know that I am God....
Psalms 46:10. Find a quiet place away from
all the noise of the world. Reach out to God
and seek His Presence with you.

Listen for that small, still voice of guidance.
Listen for God's whisper: *"This is the way; walk in it."*
God will gently nudge you on the right path.

Tap into the Love...

Prayer: Father God, help me to recognize Your voice
and know without a doubt that You are leading me
in the right direction. Help me to listen for Your
whispers of love and guidance. Amen

Notes & Reflections

Day 19

*"I know that there is nothing better for people than
to be happy and to do good while they live. That each
of them may eat and drink and find satisfaction in all
their toil—this is the gift of God."*
Ecclesiastes 3:12-13

A Gift

God wants us to be happy and to find satisfaction
in all that we do. Jesus came so we could do exactly
that. Enjoy our life through Him.

In John 8:44, the Scriptures tell us that Satan is the
father of lies. He tells lies to make us feel guilty
and not worthy of God's love. But God wants us to be
happy and to live life to the fullest.

We have all been dealt a different hand in life. And
whatever hand we were dealt, God wants us to make the
most of it and to enjoy it. And while you are enjoying your
life, remember to do something good for someone each day,
because to be happy and to do good is a gift from God.

Tap into the Love...

Prayer: Father God, thank you for the gift of happiness
and satisfaction. Thank you for such amazing
love toward us. Amen.

Notes & Reflections

Day 20

"For you created my inmost being; you knit me together in my mother's womb. I praise you because I am fearfully and wonderfully made...."
Psalms 139: 13-14

The Great Physician

The science of medicine and medical technology come from God, the creator of all things. Our Creator also gives us bodies that heal from treatments of the medical world because we are wonderfully made.

There is also the miracle healings that come from our Lord Jesus Christ. *"Praise the Lord, my soul, and forget not all his benefits—who forgives all your sins and heals all your diseases..."* Psalms 103:2-3.

Trust in the Lord Jesus, the great Physician. He can miraculously heal you, or He can heal you through others with whom He has blessed with the technology and knowledge of medicines. Either way, to God be the Glory!

Tap into the Love...

Prayer: Lord Jesus, you are the great Physician who can heal body, mind, and soul. Heal me with whatever means you see fit. I believe in the healing power of Jesus. Amen.

Notes & Reflections

Day 21

"Do you not know that your bodies are temples
of the Holy Spirit, who is in you, whom you
have received from God?"
1 Corinthians 6:19

The Temple of the Holy Spirit

Health is one of our biggest assets. The worst thing about
losing our health is that we can lose the potential for
fulfilling God's purpose and plan for our life.

We have a responsibility to take care of our bodies.
Be inquisitive. Research healthy options to maintain
your body. The Bible says, *"...the truth will set you free"*
John 8:32. Free from sickness and diseases.
Free from a path of destruction.

Ask the Holy Spirit to help you do the right things
to be on a healthy path. Eat healthy foods in moderation.
Exercise your body in a way that is of service
to the Lord and others. See your
body as a temple of the Holy Spirit.

Tap into the Love...

Prayer: Lord God, help me to see food and exercise with
a different attitude. Good health is essential to accomplish
your purpose. I want to be my best for your glory. Amen

Notes & Reflections

Day 22

*"Therefore, I tell you, do not worry about your life,
what you will eat or drink; or about your body,
what you will wear. Is not life more than food,
and the body more than clothes?"*
Matthew 6:25

Financial Woes

You may find yourself full of anxiety and fearful
about your financial situation. Will there be enough
money for food, clothes and bills?

God says to us, *"Look at the birds of the air; they do not
sow or reap or store away in barns, and yet your
heavenly Father feeds them. Are you not much
more valuable than they?"* Matthew 6:26

By turning to God in prayer, you are activating your
faith in the One who really cares. This act of faith
will undoubtedly bring you closer in your
relationship to a loving God.

Tap into the Love...

Prayer: Caring God, thank you for the assurance from your
Word, *"Before they call, I will answer; while they
are still speaking, I will hear"* Isaiah 65:24. Amen

Notes & Reflections

Day 23

"May the God of hope fill you with all joy and peace as you trust in him, so that you may overflow with hope by the power of the Holy Spirit."
Romans 15:13

Joy Magnet

Have you noticed that smiling people are contagious? You will find yourself smiling back at them. People are drawn to those who have a genuine joy, especially if it's consistent. They desire that joy for themselves.

When you truly trust in the Lord, God will fill your heart with joy, peace, hope, and *even* strength that cannot be explained. *"....the joy of the Lord is your strength"* Nehemiah 8:10.

You will draw people to you like a magnet by radiating the joy and love of Christ. Those around you will want to experience what only Jesus Christ can provide. Share the joy. Point them to Jesus.

Tap into the Love...

Prayer: Father God, help me to draw others to a place where they can know Your amazing love. May they experience for themselves the joy, peace, hope and even strength that you provide through the power of the Holy Spirit. Amen

Notes & Reflections

Day 24

"Be completely humble and gentle, be patient,
bearing with one another in love."
Ephesians 4:2

Caregiving—A Noble Task

As life advances and those we love are fast approaching the
end of their journey, we should be compelled to give extra
love and attention to them and their needs.

Caregiving is very emotionally and physically
draining. We are overwhelmed with the
responsibilities and lack of patience. The Scriptures
say that love *"....always protects, always trust,*
always hopes, always perseveres.
Love never fails" 1 Corinthians 13:7-8.

As you spend precious time with your loved one,
be patient with them. Give them respect and honor
as you would unto the Lord. Not only will it please
your Heavenly Father, but you will cherish
those memories forever.

Tap into the Love...

Prayer: Loving God, help me to see that you can turn
difficult situations or goodbyes into something
beautiful and good because of Your love for us. Amen

Notes & Reflections

Day 25

*"Now you are the body of Christ, and each
one of you is a part of it."*
I Corinthians 12:27

Diversity But Unity

Aren't you glad that everyone is not alike? Thank God for
variety by making us all unique and different. But
sometimes our differences cause strife and division.

Jesus compared the different physical body parts to the
different spiritual parts of the Body of Christ. Read 1st
Corinthians Chapter 12. We all have certain gifts and talents
to complete God's purpose for His Kingdom.

What part of the Body are you? What are your gifts and
talents? Ask God where you belong within the Body
of Christ. Work with the other members of the Body
to do good and to expand the work of God.

Tap into the Love...

Prayer: Father God, help us to know that our world of
diversity has a purpose in Your plan. Help us to unify and
set our differences aside for the cause of Jesus Christ and
what He did for us at the Cross. Amen

Notes & Reflections

Day 26

"My Father's house has many rooms; if that were not so, would I have told you that I am going there to prepare a place for you?"
John 14:2

Not Home Yet

Do you ever have a deep longing in which life doesn't seem to satisfy? Wealth, careers, health and good relationships all give us some point of satisfaction. But deep down in the soul, there is a longing for something more.

God created us for Himself. That longing will never be fulfilled until we are with Him in eternity. Perhaps David in Psalms73:25 said it well, *"Whom have I in heaven but you? And earth has nothing I desire besides you."*

The Bible tells us that our earthy home is just temporal. It tells us not to conform to the world because we are not of the world. Jesus is coming back for us. Encourage one another with these words.

Tap into the Love…

Prayer: Dear Lord, for those days that I'm longing for more than the world can offer, help me to know that longing is for You, Lord. Fill my heart with an extra portion of Your love and hope that one day You are coming back for me. Amen.

Notes & Reflections

Day 27

"Therefore, put on the full armor of God, so that when the day of evil comes, you may be able to stand your ground, and after you have done everything, to stand." Ephesians 6:13

Stand Firm

Be prepared for the everyday spiritual battles you will encounter. Satan and his demons are roaming to attack anyone who is off guard.
Be aware, ready, strong, and courageous.

Ephesians 6:14-17 describes the full armor of God. The belt of truth, the breastplate of righteousness, the shield of faith, the helmet of salvation, and the sword of the Spirit, which is the Word of God.

Be confident when you wear the full armor. Victory is found in Jesus, and He will help you fight your battles. Do all you can do to stand your ground, and after everything, to stand.

Tap into the Love...

Prayer: Dear Father God, thank you for helping me with my battles. When opposition attacks my faith, help me to hold on tight and to stand firm. I claim the power and victory through Jesus Christ, my Lord. Amen.

Notes & Reflections

Day 28

"Glory in his holy name; let the hearts of those who seek the Lord rejoice. Look to the Lord and his strength; seek his face always."
1 Chronicles 16:10-11

Seek God's Continual Presence

The Bible tells us that those who seek God *will find Him.* We are privileged through the blood of Christ to experience the Presence of the Lord God Almighty by the Holy Spirit who lives within us.

But there is a prerequisite before you can come to that special place. We need to humble our hearts and be repentant. *"Search me, God, and know my heart; test me and know my anxious thoughts. See if there is any offensive way in me..."* Psalms 139:23-24.

As you seek God's face, the Lord may reveal Himself to you in ways that will be hard to explain to the world. But without a doubt you will know that you have been in the Presence of the Lord. Seek His continual Presence.

Tap into the Love...

Prayer: Dear Father God, thank you that I can know and experience Your Holy Presence with me every day. Amen.

Notes & Reflections

Day 29

*"...now I know in part; then I shall know fully, even as I
am fully known. And now these three remain: faith,
hope and love. But the greatest of these is love."*
1 Corinthians 13:12-13

What Really Matters to God

As Christ followers, we are all going through a process of
transformation. The love of God is revealed to us in parts.
Our goal is to become more and more like Christ.

Jesus was asked the question, from all the commandments,
which one is the most important? Jesus answered,
*"Love the Lord your God with all your heart, mind,
soul, and strength. And second is this to love
your neighbor as yourself"* (Mark 12:30-31).

As we change more into the image of Jesus Christ,
we begin to see our neighbor more clearly through the
eyes of Christ. In time, we will begin to see
what really matters to God.

Tap into the Love...

Prayer: Father God, forgive me for not loving you with all
my heart and loving my neighbor as myself. Help me to
love with a love that comes from Your Heart. Amen.

Notes & Reflections

Day 30

*"It is done. I am the Alpha and the Omega, the
Beginning and the End....Those who are victorious
will inherit all this, and I will be their God
and they will be my children."*
Revelation 21:6-7

Most Holy and Praiseworthy

Is there any doubt of the love that God has for you?
He has proven His love through His Son, Jesus Christ.
This is TRUE love. Not that we loved God,
but that God loved us FIRST.

God is worthy to receive glory and honor and power.
Psalms 150:6, *"Let everything that has breath
praise the Lord."* He is the most Holy and Praiseworthy.

Praise the Lord with all that is within you first thing
in the morning for His loving kindness and faithfulness.
Praise Him during the day for His strength and guidance.
Praise Him at bedtime for His grace and forgiveness.

Tap into the Love...

Prayer: Father God, Your Word proclaims, *"Holy,
Holy, Holy is the Lord God Almighty; Who Was, and Is,
And Is to Come"* Revelation 4:8. Thank you that as a
child of God, I can join in with the choir of praise. Amen.

About the Author

Linda loves to write devotionals about everyday living through her insights and personal experiences. It is her mission to share God's Word through her writings. She has posted many of her thoughts and prayers through social media. That is where her first book, *Tapping into the Source* originated. It was a compilation of mini devotions, mostly of which she had posted on her Facebook page.

Linda has written numerous devotions and stories for newspaper publications, magazines, and church publications. She also enjoys writing children's stories. She has written the books: *Rocket Sleigh for Santa, Santa's Cookie Christmas,* and *Mister Tubby's Lemonade Stand.* She has a heart to share the beauty of life with children and to promote good, clean fun with a positive message.

Linda lives with her husband in Spring Hill, TN. They have two children and six grandchildren. Linda enjoys family time and the outdoors. She gets many of her ideas or inspirations while sitting outdoors enjoying the beautiful world that God has created.

Go to Linda's website www.lindajbwilliford.com to learn more about her upcoming devotionals and children's books. Books are available through Amazon.com

www.ingramcontent.com/pod-product-compliance
Lightning Source LLC
Chambersburg PA
CBHW071635040426
42452CB00009B/1642